MEOW!

ISBN: 978-1-64030-385-0

YOU HAD ME AT
meow

new seasons®

I swear the fish was this big!

I want to turn over a new leaf...
or eat one,
and I just can't decide which.

I don't purr.

I'm not being lazy. I'm reducing my carbon footprint.

Don't even think about it.

I SAID I have a HEADACHE!

Who you callin' fat?

Now I understand
why we have a dog....

I had fun once.

It was awful.

Every cat deserves
two fur coats in her life.

Talk to me after
I've had my coffee.

This stuff comes in a glass?
Intriguing...

Did you forget I have allergies?

It's just what happens when
you go to St. Maarten without me.

I'm going to close my eyes,
and when I open them I hope
there's a feather toy in front of me.

For your sake.

Always a bridesmaid...
never a bride.

Keeping calm and carrying on.

I hate housework.

Here's lookin' at you, jerk.

Yes, this is an
excellent vintage...
room temperature
with a hint of catnip.

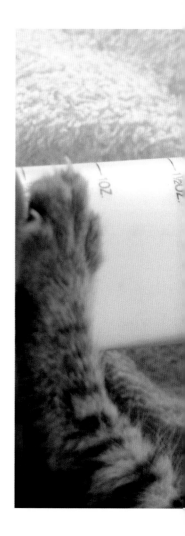

Don't even get me started.

Half the time I'm not exactly sure how I get up here either.

Did she just ask me to fetch something?
The audacity...

What does a guy have to do
to get a drink around here?

Your feathery antics are no match
for my feline prowess!

And she calls me a bitch?

What is that?

There are no feathers. No bells.

What do you do with it?

Yes. I'm pouting.

In hindsight, this wasn't a good idea.

I know the answer!

The puppy did it!

Then is it good luck if I cross your path?

Find your place in the sun. Then take a nap.

Born to be fuzzy.

Curiosity did what to the cat?

BATH is a four-letter word....

Catnap in my cat hammock.

Now I have you in my clutches!

Kitten attack!

Window shade pull string.
Challenge accepted!

I must show the leafy vine who's boss!

Indoor cat, I am an INDOOR cat!

What is THAT?

Puss in boot!

Hello, lunch.

Does this fur make me look fat?

You had me at meow.

How many dogs does it take
to screw in a light bulb?
All of 'em.
One to turn it, and the rest to
run around in circles and bark at it!

Hard day. Hair ball. Nuff said.

I'm having a bad whisker day....

Ok. So I might be a scaredy-cat.

Jimmy's Fish Market?

Do you deliver?

If one more person says
"hang in there, baby..."

With special thanks to:
Jennifer Barney, Karen Hartman, Anne O'Connor,
Frank Putrino, Anita Remijas, Barbara Rittenhouse, Mimi Roeder,
Kathleen Rose, Helene Shapiro, Patty Sprague, Linda Weber, Leslie Weyhrich

Photography © Jupiterimages Corporation, Media Bakery,
Shutterstock.com, SuperStock, Thinkstock